Authors	Karen Brown and Holly Engel
Editor	Deneen Celecia
Assistant Editor	Linda Milliken
Designer	Wendy Loreen
Illustrator	Barb Lorseyedi

About the Authors

Karen Brown has been a teacher for seventeen years. She has taught learning disabled and elementary students in Lee's Summit, Missouri. Karen has been a finalist in the Lee's Summit Teacher of the Year program. She is a member of the National Education Association, International Reading Association and Society of Children's Book Writers and Illustrators.

Holly Engel earned her Bachelor of Arts degree from Rockhurst College in Kansas City, Missouri. She has taught elementary students in the Kansas City area for four years. Holly has written articles for local publications, sharing her innovative classroom programs with the community and her peers. Currently, she is working on a masters degree specializing in reading. She is also a member of the National Education Association.

Reproducible for classroom use only.
Not for use by an entire school or school system.

© 1995 **EDUPRESS** • P.O. Box 883 • Dana Point, CA 92629

ISBN 1-56472-046-2

Table of Contents

Literature List

- ## Castles
by Beth Smith; Watts LB 1988. (5-7)
Castle history and construction are explained with details on how they changed.

- ## Walter Dragun's Town: Crafts and Trade in the Middle Ages
by Sheila Sancha; Harper LB 1988. (5-7)
Reconstruction of the life of artisans and tradespeople in 13th century England.

- ## Medieval Cathedral
by Fiona Macdonald; Bedrick 1991. (3-6)
Explains how cathedrals were built and the role they played in medieval life.

- ## Knight
by Christopher Gravett; Eyewitness Books 1993. (4-8)
Traces the history of knighthood from the 9th to the 17th century.

- ## Fourteenth-Century Towns
by John D. Clare; Harcourt 1993. (3-6)
Life in a medieval town is portrayed with illustrations and text.

- ## Life in a Medieval Village
by Gwyneth Morgan; Harper 1991. (5-7)
A story of activities in a medieval village and the effects of the church on medieval life.

- ## The Legend of King Arthur
by Alan Baker; Doubleday 1990. (4-6)
Merlin narrates the story of Arthur from his birth at Tintagel to his death.

- ## A Medieval Feast
by Aliki; Harper LB 1983. (3-6)
A visit from the king provides the occasion for a well-described feast.

- ## Merlin Dreams
by Alan Lee; Delacorte 1988. (4-6)
Nine enchanting medieval tales from the mind of a dreaming Merlin.

- ## Nicobobinus
by Terry Jones; Bedrick 1986. (5-7)
A medieval boy and his friend go to the Land of the Dragons to seek a cure for his foot.

- ## A Connecticut Yankee in King Arthur's Court
by Mark Twain; Morrow 1988. (5-7)
Story of an American who travels through time to Arthurian England.

- ## Sir Gawain and the Loathly Lady
by Selina Taylor, reteller; Lothrop 1987. (5-7)
Sir Gawain honors a pledge and breaks a spell to release a beautiful woman.

- ## Illuminations
by Jonathan Hunt; Macmillan 1989. (3-4)
Illuminated letters of the alphabet introduce different aspects of medieval life.

- ## Castles
by Rachel Wright; Watts LB 1992. (3-6)
Explore the history of castles with projects such as building a castle or making a tapestry.

- ## Knights
by Rachel Wright; Watts LB 1992 (3-6)
Make stained glass windows and a castle with easy-to-find materials.

- ## Looking into the Middle Ages
by Huck Scarry; Harper 1985. (4-6)
A pop-up book that illustrates castles, cathedrals and jousting tournaments.

EYEWITNESS BOOKS: CASTLE
by Christopher Gravett
Published by Alfred A. Knopf/Random House, 1994.
Canadian distribution by Random House of Canada Limited.

DESCRIPTION:

64 pages
Nonfiction picture book

READING LEVEL:

Read aloud—Grades 4-5
Independent—Grades 6-7

CONTENT NOTES:

Photographs of archaeological findings and authentic reproductions are teamed with detailed diagrams to provide a visual trip back in time. Easy-to-understand historical information and photo captions provide a detailed look at medieval life. Look also for *Eyewitness Books: Knight*, another medieval times title in the Eyewitness Books series which effectively brings the museum to your classroom.

CONTENT SUMMARY:

Learn about medieval castle life through text and photos. Twenty-eight, two-page units of study introduce the reader into a variety of related topics.

Follow the progression of castle construction, from the earliest development of stone fortresses to the building of concentric castles in the thirteenth century. Learn about the tools and trades involved in the construction and the defensive features of castle homes.

Examine the early weaponry and find out about the men who laid siege to the castle and its inhabitants and those who defended them.

Go inside the castle to learn about the people who lived there. Tour the kitchen and feast on exotic puddings and fowl; Step into the great hall where the hub of castle life took place; Be entertained by jesters and minstrels; Eavesdrop on the lords, ladies and children to find out how their days were spent.

Compare castles throughout medieval Europe and trace the decline of these formidable homes.

Respond

EYEWITNESS BOOKS: CASTLE

SUMMARY OF RESPONSE:
Participate in a pre-reading strategy by creating and completing a KWL chart (Know, Want To Know, Learned) about medieval times.

OBJECTIVE:
- The student will answer questions about medieval times based on information previously learned.
- The student will research to determine accuracy of previously-learned information.

THINKING LEVEL:
- Knowledge

- Comprehension

MATERIALS:
- Three pieces of butcher paper
- Marking pens
- Tape
- Table of Contents from the literature selection

PREPARATION:
- Label the top of each strip of chart paper: **Know, Want To Know, Learned.**
- Tape the chart paper to the classroom wall.

RESPONSE INSTRUCTIONS:
One by one, read aloud the sections in the table of contents. After each, allow time for students to share the information they already know, or think they know, about the topic. Record the responses on the paper labeled **Know.**

Next, students indicate an area of particular interest and specific questions they may have about that topic. List these on the **Want To Know** paper. Divide into similar-interest groups to research and find answers.

When fact-gathering is complete, gather as a class to record findings on the **Learned** paper.

Compare **Learned** information with **Know** responses. Students evaluate the accuracy of their original responses.

EVALUATION:
Is the student able to research in order to find evidence to support an answer? Is the student able to compare and evaluate the accuracy of prior information?

Respond

EYEWITNESS BOOKS: CASTLE

SUMMARY OF RESPONSE:
Play a problem-solving game that depicts the responsibilities of people living in a castle.

OBJECTIVE:
- The student will use acquired knowledge to accurately simulate the role of a person in the castle.
- The student will demonstrate problem-solving abilities based on literature content.

THINKING LEVEL:
- Synthesis
- Comprehension

MATERIALS:
- Job Cards, following
- Problem Cards, following

PREPARATION:
- Reproduce a copy of the Job and Problem Cards for each group.
- Cut out the Job Cards and Problem Cards for each group.
- Divide into groups of six students.

RESPONSE INSTRUCTIONS:
Each member of the group draws a job card which indicates their position in the castle. They tell what their role will be.

A problem card is drawn by the lord of the castle who must delegate the problem to the appropriate worker. The worker proposes how they would solve the problem. The other members of the group decide on whether the idea is authentic for that time period. The lord selects another problem to assign to the appropriate worker. Continue as time permits.

EVALUATION:
Can students assume the role of a worker in a castle? Can students think of solutions that are appropriate to that time period?

EYEWITNESS BOOKS: CASTLE
JOB CARDS

Lord
Owner of the castle

Castellan
Looks after the building and defenses

Marshal
Supervises horses, soldiers and outside servant

Garrison/Knight
Soldiers defending the castle

Chamberlain
Oversees food and drink

Steward
Runs the finances and estates

PROBLEM CARDS

The horses are out of food and the castle is under siege.

The Lord wishes to install a different drawbridge. He wants it as soon as possible. It is a time of peace.

One of the servants has not been showing up to work in the kitchen. This has happened for three consecutive days.

The castle is under fire. The garrisons are running low on arrows. There are not enough crossbows.

The castellan falls ill. There are no battles presently, but word has it that there could be one soon.

A child of the Lord is throwing wood and rocks into the moat. He's been doing this on many different occasions.

EYEWITNESS BOOKS: CASTLE

SUMMARY OF RESPONSE:
Complete a vocabulary grid using terms from the literature selection.

OBJECTIVE:
• Given a list of definitions, the student will match it to the correct vocabulary word.
• The students will learn to use number coordinates on a grid.

THINKING LEVEL:
• Comprehension

• Application

MATERIALS:
• Pencil
• Vocabulary Grid, following
• Dictionaries

PREPARATION:
• Reduce a copy of the Vocabulary Grid for each student.
• Determine if you wish for the students to work individually, in pairs or small groups.
• Decide if you want them to use dictionaries or the glossaries of other texts.

Answer Key

	1	2	3	4	5	6	7	8	9	10	11	12	13	14
16							C							
15					m	O	T	T	E					
14							n						S	
13							C				m	O	A	T
12				K	E	E	P					R		
11							n					T		
10				P	O	R	T	C	U	L	L	I	S	
9		B					R					E		
8	D	R	A	W	B	R	I	G	E			S		
7		I					C		A					
6		L							R					
5		E							R					
4		Y							I					
3							C	A	S	T	L	E		
2									O					
1	C	A	S	T	E	L	L	A	n					

RESPONSE INSTRUCTIONS:
Discuss the purpose and components of a number grid. Review vocabulary words introduced during the reading of the selected title.

When the review is sufficient, provide a copy of the vocabulary grid and ask students to complete the grid by reading the definitions and locating the correct word in the dictionary.

ACROSS

[12, 5]	KEEP	[3, 7]	CASTLE	
[8, 1]	DRAWBRIDGE	[10, 4]	PORTCULLIS	
[1, 1]	CASTELLAN	[13, 11]	MOAT	
[15, 6]	MOTTE			

DOWN

[14, 12]	SORTIES
[9, 3]	BAILEY
[16, 7]	CONCENTRIC
[8, 9]	GARRISON

EVALUATION:
Is the student able to match vocabulary words with their definitions? Does the student learn and understand how to use a number grid correctly?

EYEWITNESS BOOKS: CASTLE
Vocabulary Grid

Directions: Read the number pairs. These are also called *number coordinates*. The first number in the pair is found by counting up the grid. The second number is found by counting across from the position of the first number on the grid. Write a letter in each box. If the clue is in the ACROSS list, write the letters across horizontally. If clue is in the DOWN list, write letters down, vertically. The first one ACROSS is done for you.

ACROSS

[12, 5]   Round tower where nobleman's family lived.
[8, 1]   Path across a moat that can be raised or lowered.
[1, 1]   Runs castle in lord's absence.
[15, 6]   An earth mound.
[3, 7]   Fortified private residence of a lord.

[10, 4]   Heavy, iron gate.
[13, 11]   A ditch around a castle.

DOWN

[14, 12]   Surprise attacks.
[9, 3]   The yard around the castle.
[16, 7]   Rings of walls inside the other.
[8, 9]   Body of soldiers defending a castle.

The grid: rows labeled 1–16 (bottom to top), columns labeled 1–14 (left to right). At row 12, columns 5–8 contain the letters: K E E P

Respond

EYEWITNESS BOOKS: CASTLE

SUMMARY OF RESPONSE:
Compile a Venn diagram to determine whether there are more similarities or differences between castles of different countries.

OBJECTIVE:
- The student will list similarities or differences between castles of different countries in a Venn diagram.
- The student will recall specific features of a country's castles.

THINKING LEVEL:
- Synthesis

- Knowledge

MATERIALS:
- Chart paper
- Markers

PREPARATION:
- Students are divided into four equal groups.
- Teacher gathers other resources that might show and tell about the castles of the four countries.
- Reproduce copies of pages 14-21 and pages 36-37 from the literature selection for reference.

RESPONSE INSTRUCTIONS:
The students research the castles of their chosen country: France, Germany, Spain or Japan. Each group notates important features, style, characteristics and history of their castles.

When research is complete, the groups meet with another group and compile a Venn diagram (see illustration at right) to create a visual chart that shows how the castles are alike or different. The groups switch and make another list of similarities and differences between the castles. Continue until all comparisons are complete.

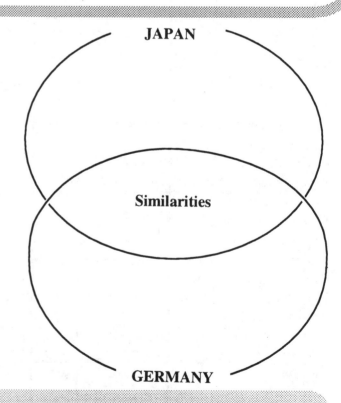

EVALUATION:
Is the student able to describe the castles of a country? Can the castles be compared and contrasted with another country's through use of a Venn diagram?

Respond

EYEWITNESS BOOKS: CASTLE

SUMMARY OF RESPONSE:
Develop a real estate advertisement that depicts the features of a medieval castle.

OBJECTIVE:
- The student will identify features of various types of medieval castles.
- The student will depict the important features of a medieval castle in the form of a real estate advertisement.

THINKING LEVEL:
- Comprehension
- Synthesis

MATERIALS:
- White construction paper
- Pen or pencil
- Crayons
- Newspapers or other publications containing real estate advertisements

PREPARATION:
- Review the elements in a real estate advertisement.

RESPONSE INSTRUCTIONS:
Students individually skim the text to record the dates and features of the various types of medieval castles. For example:

earth and timber—9th century
ringwork—10th century
motte-and-bailey—11th century
great towers or donjons—11th century
Crusader castles—12th century
concentric castles—13th century

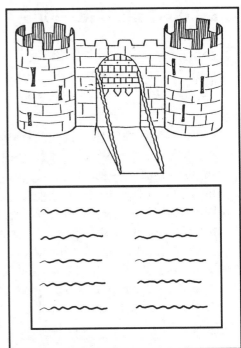

Upon studying the variety in castle styles, the student will select one to sell in a real estate advertisement published **during** medieval times. The appealing features should be highlighted along with information about the castle's construction.

This information should be presented on one half of the construction paper. A drawing of the castle should be made on the other half.

EVALUATION:
Can the student correctly write an advertisement that correctly depicts the important features of a medieval castle?

EYEWITNESS BOOKS: CASTLE

SUMMARY OF RESPONSE:
Conduct cooperative research which is later taught to other students using the "Jig Saw" approach.

OBJECTIVE:
• The student will research and find answers to questions about medieval castles.
• The student will teach this information to other students.

THINKING LEVEL:
• Application

• Comprehension

MATERIALS:
• Notebook paper
• Pencil/pen
• Additional resource books
• Research Starter Cards, following

PREPARATION:
• Determine home groups for each student.
• Cut apart the Research Starter Cards.
• Gather other books which may be helpful in answering these questions.
• Compile a short test about important facts from the book.

RESPONSE INSTRUCTIONS:
Assign each student to a "home" group with five to six members. Each child in the home group is given a number. Home groups split into research groups according to their number. Give each group a research starter card:

• **Foods**	• **Games**	• **Tools**	• **Religion**
• **Arts**	• **Jobs**	• **Clothing**	• **Buildings**

When studying has been completed in the research groups, home groups reunite. Each student is responsible for teaching their area of expertise to the other members of the group. A test can be given to the whole class, and the highest score in the group will be averaged with the lowest score for assessment purposes. An essay test may give the teacher the most valuable information about the success of this approach.

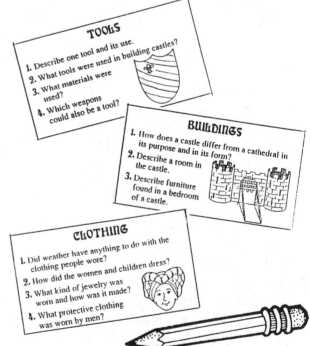

TOOLS
1. Describe one tool and its use.
2. What tools were used in building castles?
3. What materials were used?
4. Which weapons could also be a tool?

BUILDINGS
1. How does a castle differ from a cathedral in its purpose and in its form?
2. Describe a room in the castle.
3. Describe furniture found in a bedroom of a castle.

CLOTHING
1. Did weather have anything to do with the clothing people wore?
2. How did the women and children dress?
3. What kind of jewelry was worn and how was it made?
4. What protective clothing was worn by men?

EVALUATION:
Is the student able to successfully teach learned information to other classmates?

EYEWITNESS BOOKS: CASTLE
Research Starter Cards

FOODS

1. Make a list of five different foods eaten.
2. What did they have to drink?
3. How did the people get the food they ate?
4. What utensils were used to cook and eat with?

ARTS

1. Choose a musical instrument to describe.
2. Where would you find examples of medieval art?
3. Describe a family flag, shield or medallion.
4. What forms of exercise were popular?

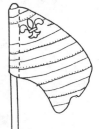

GAMES

1. What sports were enjoyed in medieval times?
2. Find the name of a board game and describe it.
3. What festivals were celebrated?
4. Describe a knights' tournament.

TOOLS

1. Describe one tool and its use.
2. What tools were used in building castles?
3. What materials were used?
4. Which weapons could also be a tool?

RELIGION

1. What religion was practiced during this time period?
2. List two gods or goddesses and tell why they were worshipped.
3. Who were the lords and how did they obtain their status?

JOBS

1. Why was a castellan important?
2. Describe a duty of a castle builder.
3. What was the job of the steward?
4. How do the jobs of marshall and chamberlain differ?

CLOTHING

1. Did weather have anything to do with the clothing people wore?
2. How did the women and children dress?
3. What kind of jewelry was worn and how was it made?
4. What protective clothing was worn by men?

BUILDINGS

1. How does a castle differ from a cathedral in its purpose and in its form?
2. Describe a room in the castle.
3. Describe furniture found in a bedroom of a castle.

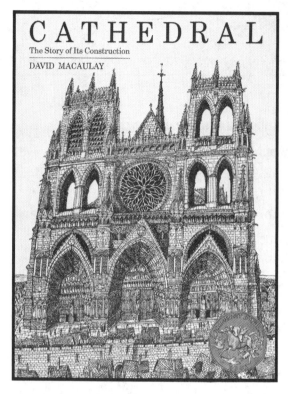

CATHEDRAL: The Story of Its Construction

by David Macaulay

Published by Houghton Mifflin, 1973.

Canadian distribution by Thomas Allen & Son, Limited.

DESCRIPTION:

80 pages

Picture book

READING LEVEL:

Read aloud—Grades 4-6

Independent—Grades 6-7

CONTENT NOTES:

This Caldecott Honor Book is illustrated with detailed pen-and-ink illustrations. The cathedral is imaginary, but the story behind its construction and the details presented are based on historical facts. Also included is a glossary of terms that provides the reader with a summary of content-related vocabulary.

CONTENT SUMMARY:

From the commission of the clergymen and bishop to the completion of the cathedral 86 years later, the building of a cathedral to provide a place of worship and a resting place for the remains of a knight is documented in story form.

Learn reasons behind the construction and meet the original architect who designs this sacred building. The building process continues with the clearing of land, the excavation for the foundation, the shaping and transportation of stones and, finally, the rising of the spire.

Meet the people—stone cutters, bishops, masons, carpenters, glassmakers and blacksmiths—who enabled the bishop's request to become reality.

Interesting and remarkable facts about the inventive methods and tools utilized in this massive undertaking are included throughout the text.

CATHEDRAL: The Story of Its Construction

SUMMARY OF RESPONSE:
Make a chart that compares the tools used to build cathedrals during the Middle Ages with tools used in modern-day construction.

OBJECTIVE:
- The student will identify purposes of tools used in building a cathedral.
- The student will compare tools used in medieval times with tools used in present day.
- The student will invent a tool that will speed up the process of building a cathedral.

THINKING LEVEL:
- Analysis

- Synthesis

- Synthesis

MATERIALS:
- Chart paper
- Markers
- Samples of tools or tool catalogs

PREPARATION:
- Divide the class into cooperative groups.
- Reproduce pages 10-11 of the literature selection and distribute one to each group.
- Share tools brought from home and review tool catalogs.

RESPONSE INSTRUCTIONS:
Students examine the pictures of tools used in building a cathedral. They should determine the use of each of the tools and record their conclusions on chart paper. This information is presented and explained to the rest of the class. Similarities and differences between groups will be discussed. The class decides on the best use for each tool.

Now the students list tools that currently exist. Compile a list of similarities and differences between medieval and modern tools. Functions and features need to be evaluated. How would these tools have helped the medieval people?

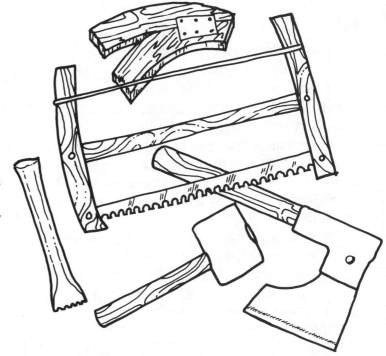

EVALUATION:
Is the student able to determine functions of tools used in building cathedrals? Is the student able to compare and contrast historical tools with present day ones?

CATHEDRAL: The Story of Its Construction

SUMMARY OF RESPONSE:
Work in cooperative groups to develop a sequential chart that recalls the steps in the building of a cathedral as portrayed in the literature selection.

OBJECTIVE:
- The student will sequence the steps in building a cathedral.
- The student will work cooperatively in a decision-making process.

THINKING LEVEL:
- Knowledge
- Evaluation

MATERIALS:
- Sequence Strips, following
- Scissors
- Pen or pencil
- Glue or tape
- Poster board or construction paper

PREPARATION:
- Assign cooperative groups of three students.
- Reproduce a copy of the Sequence Strips for each group.
- Provide a poster board or large sheets of construction paper for each group.

RESPONSE INSTRUCTIONS:
Cut apart the sequence strips and spread them on the floor or table so that each group member can see them clearly. Read each sentence silently or take turns reading them aloud.

Work together to determine the most accurate sequence of events and arrange the sentence strips, top to bottom, on the poster board or construction paper. Students must rely on memory. They may not peek in the book for answers.

Once the order has been agreed upon, glue or tape the strips to the poster board. Draw an outline of a cathedral around the arranged strips. Each team that completes the task accurately earns the title of *Master Architects* for the rest of the day.

Stones are dug out of the quarry, cut, chiseled and hammered to the correct pattern.

Timber is cut for the building of the scaffolding and workshops.

EVALUATION:
Is the student able to sequence the events accurately? Is the student able to work with other students in a cooperative manner using a decision-making process?

CATHEDRAL: The Story of Its Construction

Sequence Strips

A great procession celebrates the completion of the cathedral.	Stones are dug out of the quarry, cut, chiseled and hammered to the correct pattern.
Stones are layered to form the foundation.	Vaulted ceilings are constructed.
There is a break in the stonework due to cold weather.	The roof is made up of a series of triangular frames.
The architect settles on a final design and sketches it.	The bells, rose window and sculptures are put into place.
The walls of the choir are constructed in three stages.	Timber is cut for the building of the scaffolding and workshops.
Colored glass for the windows are installed.	A maze pattern of stone slabs is created in the floor.
The site of the cathedral is cleared.	Master craftsmen are hired to work under the architect.
Buttresses are erected.	The walls are built above the foundation.
An architect is hired.	Workshops are built so work can continue during bad weather.
The spire is erected and the doors are finished and installed.	Four large bells are cast in bronze.
The drain pipes, down spouts and gutters are cast.	The hole for the foundation is dug.
The original architect dies.	Specific tools are made for the construction of the cathedral.

CATHEDRAL: The Story of Its Construction

SUMMARY OF RESPONSE:
Form mutual-interest groups to complete a research questionnaire about cathedrals and religious leaders of medieval times. Follow with a comparison discussion.

OBJECTIVE:
- The student will utilize research resources in order to locate information about a selected topic.
- The student will interpret and use the gathered information to answer a list of questions.
- The student will compare and contrast information to determine the historical accuracy of the literature selection.

THINKING LEVEL:
- Comprehension
- Comprehension
- Evaluation

MATERIALS:
- Encyclopedias
- Research books (see Literature List page 3)
- Research Questionnaire, following
- Index cards
- Pencils

PREPARATION:
- Gather and review research materials.
- Divide into cooperative groups according to interest. Select a secretary.
- Reproduce and distribute a questionnaire for each group.

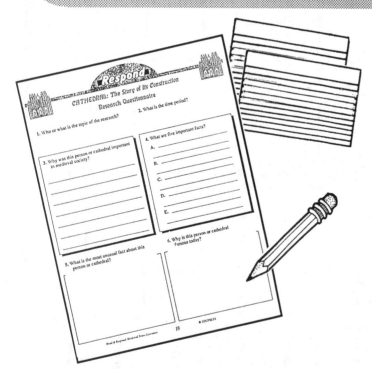

RESPONSE INSTRUCTIONS:
After selecting a medieval religious leader or cathedral, students work in mutual-interest groups to gather information and complete the research questionnaire.

Take notes individually on index cards to share with the group. Complete the research questionnaire together based upon the gathered data. The secretary may complete the final draft. Each group presents their findings to the rest of the class in an oral report.

The class then discusses whether or not the book, *Cathedral: The Story of Its Construction*, is historically accurate according to what was learned. All ideas must be defended with specific facts and statements.

EVALUATION:
Is the student able to tell where a cathedral might be seen today? Is the student able to determine nonfictional parts of the book and defend its accuracy?

CATHEDRAL: The Story of Its Construction
Research Questionnaire

1. Who or what is the topic of the research?

2. What is the time period?

3. Why was this person or cathedral important in medieval society?

_____

_____

_____

_____

_____

_____

4. What are five important facts?

A. _____

_____

B. _____

_____

C. _____

_____

D. _____

_____

E. _____

_____

5. What is the most unusual fact about this person or cathedral?

6. Why is this person or cathedral famous today?

Respond

CATHEDRAL: The Story of Its Construction

SUMMARY OF RESPONSE:
Create, draw and label a diagram for a medieval cathedral floorplan.

OBJECTIVE:
- The student will demonstrate knowledge of a cathedral's architecture by drawing a floorplan.
- The student will apply prior knowledge to add historically accurate detail to the design of the cathedral.

THINKING LEVEL:
- Synthesis
- Application

MATERIALS:
- Graph paper
- Blueprints or sample floorplans from model homes or apartments
- Pencil
- Straight edge

PREPARATION:
- Browse through books with pictures of the interior of medieval cathedrals.
- Invite a local architect to explain how to draw an accurate floorplan and what symbols might be used.

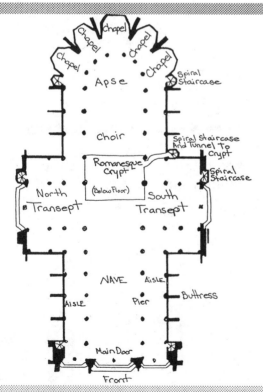

RESPONSE INSTRUCTIONS:
Brainstorm a list of architectural terms used in the literature selection. Refer also to page 12 in the literature selection. Review the elements of a diagram and how the parts of the featured subject are labeled.

Students diagram a cathedral floorplan on graph paper. Rooms should be labeled and be historically accurate. Terms shown at right need to be included.

EVALUATION:
Is the student able to use prior knowledge to create the floorplan of a cathedral? Does the student demonstrate comprehension of the elements in a diagram?

CATHEDRAL: The Story of Its Construction

SUMMARY OF RESPONSE:
Play an interactive vocabulary game that matches words from the text to their definitions.

OBJECTIVE:
- The student will match vocabulary words with definitions from literature content.

THINKING LEVEL:
- Knowledge

MATERIALS:
- Index cards
- Glossary, page 80 from literature selection
- Pencil/pen

PREPARATION:
- Divide class into teams of four to six.
- Write each word from the glossary on a separate index card.
- Create a set of cards for each team.
- Choose a student to be the reader.

RESPONSE INSTRUCTIONS:
The reader will choose, at random, a definition from the glossary to read aloud to the teams. Team members discuss and decide which word from the index cards matches the definition just read. The card is placed in front of them on the floor or table. The reader proceeds to read another definition. The team decides on a matching word card and places it below the first card selected. Definitions and responses continue until all cards are used. Answers are placed in order from top to bottom in single column. Reader keeps track of correct order and announces answers at the end. Score a point for each correct answer. Position of cards may not be changed as game proceeds.

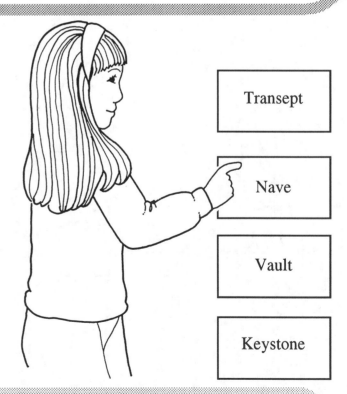

EVALUATION:
Is the student able to match the accurate word to definitions of the vocabulary words? Are students able to listen and comprehend definitions when read aloud?

CATHEDRAL: The Story of Its Construction

SUMMARY OF RESPONSE:
Play a simulation game that places students as workers on a cathedral in medieval times. Record the experience in a journal.

OBJECTIVE:
- The student will use acquired knowledge to accurately simulate the role of a cathedral builder.
- The student will record their opinion and feelings regarding their occupation.

THINKING LEVEL:
- Application
- Evaluation

MATERIALS:
- Occupation Cards, following
- Appropriate clothing (optional)
- Writing Paper
- Pencil
- Paper bag or bowl

PREPARATION:
- Reproduce and cut apart enough pages of occupation cards so that each student has a card. There should be only one architect, master mason and master quarryman.
- Put occupation cards in a bag or bowl.

RESPONSE INSTRUCTIONS:
Conduct a discussion of the workers involved in the construction of a cathedral and their individual tasks.

Each student draws an Occupation Card from the bag or bowl. Play a game that simulates the construction of a cathedral by spending the class period or the day in that role. Students keep a journal expressing emotions and reactions during the simulation. Stop several times for journal entries and to discuss how the work is progressing.

How did they respond to their supervisor? Did the work make them tired? What did they like or dislike about their role in the construction? How could their job have been made better or easier?

EVALUATION:
Can the students express their feelings about living in that time period? Can they compare and contrast that lifestyle with their own?

CATHEDRAL: The Story of Its Construction
Occupation Cards

MASTER CARPENTER Supervised the cutting of timber for the construction of scaffolding and machines.	**ARCHITECT** Designed and supervised the construction of the cathedral, from start to finish.
MASTER MASON Used a level to make sure the stones were horizontal and the wall straight.	**MASTER QUARRYMAN** Supervised fifty apprentice stone cutters and 250 laborers working to mine the stone.
METAL WORKER Designed and made the bolts, locks and hinges for the doors.	**ROOFER** Cast the drain pipes, gutters and lead sheets to cover the beams. Built the spire.
SCULPTOR Designed and carved the gutters and downspouts (gargoyles) for the exterior.	**LABORER** Demolished the old cathedral and cleared the land. Dug deep holes for the foundation.
CARPENTER Nailed the wood buttresses together. Made the scaffolding. Built the doors.	**GLASSMAKER** Blew the glass and cut it into shapes for the stained glass windows.
MORTAR-MAKER Mixed lime, water and sand to make cement for the laborers to carry to the masons.	**BLACKSMITH** Made new tools to replace old ones. Made the nails for the doors.
STONE CUTTER Cut, chiseled and hammered stone to match patterns supplied by the master mason.	**STONE MASON** Laid the stones and poured concrete to build the walls. Laid the stone floor.

SAINT GEORGE AND THE DRAGON
retold by Margaret Hodges
Published by Little, Brown and Company, 1984.
Canadian distribution by Little, Brown and Company Canada.

DESCRIPTION:
32 pages
Picture book

READING LEVEL:
Read aloud—Grades 3-4
Independent—Grades 5-6

CONTENT NOTES:
There are many book versions of the legend of the Red Cross Knight, who, as a brave dragon slayer, became known as Saint George, the patron saint of England. This version is a winner of the The Caldecott Medal. Each picture is framed with unique illustrations of vines, flowers, fairies and unicorns. Students may want to look for other versions of the legend to compare story content and illustration quality.

CONTENT SUMMARY:

A princess named Una, is fearful for the future of her kingdom. A dreadful dragon is frightening the people and laying waste to her land. She leaves to find someone who will face the dragon. Her search leads her to The Red Cross Knight. The Red Cross Knight is sent by the Queen of the Fairies to test his strength and skills against the dragon. It is his destiny to be England's patron saint, Saint George.

The knight and dragon meet in battle, with each enduring vicious blows and damaging wounds. Just when it appears that the Red Cross Knight has suffered a fatal wound and lost the battle, he finds healing power from an ancient spring. The fight continues the next day. Again, the nearly defeated knight gains strength, this time from the dew of an apple tree.

On the third day of fierce battle, the Red Cross Knight is victorious. The dragon is slain. A grateful king and queen reward the Red Cross Knight with the hand of their daughter in marriage.

SAINT GEORGE AND THE DRAGON

SUMMARY OF RESPONSE:
Students work in cooperative pairs to make page-by-page predictions about story content as you read the literature selection together.

OBJECTIVE:
- The student will use context clues and details to tell story predictions to partners.
- The student will compare predictions with actual content.

THINKING LEVEL:
- Synthesis
- Comprehension

MATERIALS:
- Literature selection
- Pen or pencil
- Writing paper

PREPARATION:
- Divide into cooperative pairs.
- Ask students to have a piece of writing paper ready for story predictions.

RESPONSE INSTRUCTIONS:
Begin by reading the first page of the book aloud and giving students time to study the illustrations. Each student writes a one or two sentence prediction about what they think will happen next in the story. Allow a few minutes for the students to share predictions with their partner.

Move on to the next page in the literature selection and read it aloud. Partners confirm or correct predictions of the previous page and write a new prediction for the next page. Repeat the sharing process.

Continue this strategy process throughout the text.

EVALUATION:
Is the student able to make predictions based on context clues and story details? Can the student compare predictions with actual text?

Respond

SAINT GEORGE AND THE DRAGON

SUMMARY OF RESPONSE:
Paint a medieval tapestry that depicts a reward presented to the dragon slayer in the story.

OBJECTIVE:
• The student will identify specific events in content.
• The student will present this information in a painted tapestry.

THINKING LEVEL:
• Knowledge
• Application

MATERIALS:
• Medieval Tapestry frame, following
• Watercolor or tempera paints
• Sample pictures of medieval tapestries from resource and art history books
• Chalk, chalkboard

PREPARATION:
• Reproduce a copy of the Medieval Tapestry frame for each student.
• Discuss the use of tapestries during the Middle Ages as artistic story-tellers of historical events.

RESPONSE INSTRUCTIONS:
Brainstorm a list of the rewards presented to Saint George, the dragon slayer, upon his defeat of the dragon. Write the list on the chalkboard. These include:

• wreaths of flowers
• tambourine music
• laurel branches laid at the hero's feet
• marriage
• gifts of gold and ivory

Depict the presentation to Saint George of one or more of these rewards with a painting in the tapestry frame. Glue the individual tapestries on a larger sheet of butcher paper to create a classroom mural, if desired.

EVALUATION:
Can the student create a historical tapestry that depicts story content?

Respond

SAINT GEORGE AND THE DRAGON

SUMMARY OF RESPONSE:
Brainstorm alternative plot directions and rewrite the legend with a different ending. Illustrate the alternative ending using the illustrative techniques in the literature selection.

OBJECTIVE:
- The student will develop possible new plot directions.
- The student will rewrite the story ending based on new plot directions.
- The student will illustrate based on a specific style.

THINKING LEVEL:
- Application
- Synthesis

- Application

MATERIALS:
- White construction paper
- Crayons or markers
- Lined writing paper
- Pen

PREPARATION:
- Complete reading the literature selection.
- Provide each student with a sheet of white construction paper. Make the literature selection available so the illustrations can be examined.

RESPONSE INSTRUCTIONS:
When you have finished reading the story, ask students to brainstorm some possible plot developments had the dragon won the battle instead of the knight. For example:
- The dragon set the village on fire.
- The dragon fell in love with Una.
- Una picked up the sword and began to fight the dragon.

Students select one of these starter sentences and rewrite the ending to the story.

When their writing is complete, students illustrate the new ending, employing the same design techniques as were used in the literature selection.

Invite authors to share their new endings and illustrations.

EVALUATION:
Can the student develop new plot paths? Can the student rewrite a new story ending? Is the student able to duplicate illustration techniques?

SAINT GEORGE AND THE DRAGON

SUMMARY OF RESPONSE:
Students and teacher will use the **reciprocal questioning** technique to develop more sophisticated question behaviors.

OBJECTIVE:
- The student will answer teacher generated questions about the text.
- The student will formulate questions to ask the teacher about the text which the teacher will answer.

THINKING LEVEL:
- Comprehension
- Recall

MATERIALS:
- Literature selection

PREPARATION:
- Complete reading the literature selection.

RESPONSE INSTRUCTIONS:
The teacher and students will take turns answering questions based on the text. Generally, the student questions will be recall questions to begin. Teacher questions should be geared to higher levels of thinking so as to model sophisticated questioning behaviors.

Requests may be made for rephrasing or clarification and the responder should often be asked to justify answers by referring back to the text.

Some "teacher" questions are provided in the box at right.

1. *Why do you think the hermit did not tell George he was "of English earth" until he was grown up?*

2. *What is your opinion of Una?*

3. *How would you defend the actions of the king and queen hiding in the castle?*

4. *Why did the main character choose to continue to fight the dragon day after day?*

5. *What significance is the illustration on the back cover?*

6. *What information would you use to support the view that George was brave?*

EVALUATION:
Can the student generate questions to be answered by the teacher? Can the student answer teacher-generated questions at higher levels of thinking?

SAINT GEORGE AND THE DRAGON

SUMMARY OF RESPONSE:
Work in cooperative groups to complete a character study questionnaire for one of the main characters in the story.

OBJECTIVE:
- The student will answer questions about the main characters.
- The student will interpret the actions of the main character in order to gain further understanding.

THINKING LEVEL:
- Comprehension
- Analysis

MATERIALS:
- Character Study Questions, following
- Pencils

PREPARATION:
- Divide class into small, cooperative groups. Select a main character—The Red Cross Knight, Una, the dragon—for each group to analyze.
- Reproduce a copy of the Character Study Questions for each group.

RESPONSE INSTRUCTIONS:
A character study questionnaire enables the students to become more involved with the main characters. The purpose of the questions is to prompt discussion about the actions of the characters that will lead to evaluative conclusions.

After the questionnaires are complete, gather as a class to compare and contrast conclusions.

EVALUATION:
Is the student able to answer questions and draw conclusions about a main character in order to better understand the actions taken in the story?

1. Is the main character someone who actually lived, could likely exist or was created for this story?

2. How does God and Heaven affect the main character?

3. Who are the other characters in the story? Did they actually live or are they fictional?

4. What does the character's speech, actions, ideas and appearance tell you about him?

5. Where do you think the main character got his strength and courage?

6. What motivates the main character to fight the dragon in this story?

7. How do the other characters feel about the main character?

8. Do you think the main character's personality, daily life or position in the community would change after his actions in the story?

9. Does the main character have an opportunity to learn anything in the story?

10. What legacy does the main character leave?

11. What sort of role model does the main character make of himself through his actions in this story?

SAINT GEORGE AND THE DRAGON

SUMMARY OF RESPONSE:
Create a "help wanted" ad in which a princess is seeking to find a brave knight to destroy a mean, powerful dragon.

OBJECTIVE:
• The student will use knowledge of personality characteristics to create a "help wanted" advertisement.
• The student will evaluate the effectiveness of the information of the completed ad.

THINKING LEVEL:
• Synthesis

• Evaluation

MATERIALS:
• Help Wanted poster, following
• Crayons or markers
• Several examples of advertisements and help wanted ads from newspapers

PREPARATION:
• Reproduce a copy of the Help Wanted poster for each student.
• Review elements found in advertisements and help wanted ads.

RESPONSE INSTRUCTIONS:
The author does not say where the princess found George. There are some unique and vital characteristics a knight needs to achieve in killing a dragon.

Using content information create a "help wanted" advertisement for a knight who is needed to slay a dragon. What words should be used to describe the kind of person wanted? Where should the applicant apply? What will the payment be? Students can make pictures and designs on their ad to grab the reader's attention.

After the help wanted ads are completed, review each one and evaluate the effectiveness of the information.

EVALUATION:
Was the student able to recall details from the book to create an advertisement? Were the elements included in the student's ad effective?

HELP WANTED

KNIGHTS OF THE ROUND TABLE
by Gwen Ross, Illustrated by Norman Green
Published by Random House, Inc. 1985.
Canadian distribution by Random House of Canada Limited.

DESCRIPTION:
110 pages
Chapter book

READING LEVEL:
Read aloud—Grades 3-4
Independent—Grades 3-6

CONTENT NOTES:
This book is one title from a series called Step into Classics™. The high interest content is written in chapter book form, for the lower level reader. Each chapter is a story within itself adapted from the popular legends about King Arthur and his Knights of the Round Table. Look for other versions about King Arthur and his knights for comparison. Look, also, for *Robin Hood*, another medieval legend adapted for the Step into Classics™ series.

CONTENT SUMMARY:

A magical tale full of dragons and wizards, *Knights of the Round Table* retells many of the legends surrounding King Arthur and his brave Knights of the Round Table who protected the kingdom of Camelot against the powers of evil.

Each chapter is a tale of its own. Find out how Arthur, hidden by the wizard, Merlin, at birth, takes his rightful place on the throne as king by pulling the magic sword, Excalibur, from a stone when no other knight of the kingdom could.

Meet Sir Lancelot, the bravest knight of all and discover how he earned his honored seat as a Knight of the Round Table.

There are riddles to solve and magic spells to be broken as King Arthur fights his wicked step sister's spells.

Ride with the brave knights as they prove their strength and worthiness to sit at the Round Table by helping the weak and battling fierce dragons and knights.

KNIGHTS OF THE ROUND TABLE

SUMMARY OF RESPONSE:
Identify a character's personality traits and use this information to compare the character with another in the literature selection.

OBJECTIVE:
- The student will identify personality traits by examining the actions of a character in the story.
- The student will support these selections with examples from story content.
- The student will evaluate and select personal traits and make a comparison with the character in the story.

THINKING LEVEL:
- Analysis
- Analysis
- Evaluation

MATERIALS:
- Pencils
- Chalk
- Chalkboard
- Index cards

PREPARATION:
- Give each student two index cards.

RESPONSE INSTRUCTIONS:
As a class, brainstorm personality traits. List them on the chalkboard. Each one may be discussed briefly. Next, recall the characters in the story and list them on the chalkboard.

When the lists are complete, each student selects one character to write on the index card. Under the name, applicable personality traits are selected and listed. Students must consider the character's actions and be prepared to support their conclusions with examples from content during classroom discussion.

Next, each student writes his/her name on an index card. They should select the personality traits they feel best describe themselves and write them on the index card. Compare personal traits with the character of choice. Save the personal cards to assist with student assessment.

honest
sensitive
trustworthy
loyal
faithful
loving

EVALUATION:
Is the student able to accurately describe a character's traits based on content information? Can the student identify personal traits and compare them to a story character?

Respond

KNIGHTS OF THE ROUND TABLE

SUMMARY OF RESPONSE:
Complete an Anticipation Guide in a pre-reading strategy that establishes a focus for reading and an activation of prior knowledge.

OBJECTIVE:
• Before reading the selection, the student will draw from personal experience to respond to statements relating to key issues in the text.
• After reading the selection, the student will respond to the same statements.
• The student will compare and analyze changes in opinion.

THINKING LEVEL:
• Evaluation

• Evaluation

• Analysis

MATERIALS:
• Anticipation Guide, following
• Pencil

PREPARATION:
• Reproduce and distribute one Anticipation Guide to each student.

RESPONSE INSTRUCTIONS:
Prior to reading the literature selection, ask the students to read each statement on the Anticipation Guide. Have them check **Agree** or **Disagree** under the BEFORE column for each statement. After each student has completed the BEFORE column, come together as a class and discuss why each student chose to agree or disagree with the statements.

After reading the literature selection, ask students to read each statement again on the Anticipation Guide. Have them check **Agree** or **Disagree** under the AFTER column. Come together again as a class and discuss any changes in opinion. What changes do students feel may be attributed to having read the literature selection and why?

EVALUATION:
Can the student respond to statements relating to key issues of the text before and after reading? Does the student participate in the class discussion about these key issues?

KNIGHTS OF THE ROUND TABLE
Anticipation Guide

BEFORE

Agree   Disagree

AFTER

Agree   Disagree

1. All men are created equal.

2. Women can do anything a man can do.

3. It is easy to be loyal to your country and its leaders.

4. Families love each member and try to take care of them.

5. It is safe to go on adventures and see the world.

6. First impressions tell everything there is to know about a person.

7. All kings must be trained from the day they are born.

8. Kings are brave, fair and honest.

9. What is beautiful is good.

10. One should always keep one's word.

KNIGHTS OF THE ROUND TABLE

SUMMARY OF RESPONSE:
Complete a story map for one knight's adventure in the literature selection; then create a second story map for a different legend about an imaginary medieval knight.

OBJECTIVE:
- The student will identify the elements of the story in order to complete a story map.
- The student will complete a second story map for a different legend of a medieval knight.

THINKING LEVEL:
- Comprehension

- Synthesis

MATERIALS:
- Story Map, following
- Pencils

PREPARATION:
- Reproduce and distribute two Story Maps for each student.
- Discuss the steps involved for its completion.

RESPONSE INSTRUCTIONS:
After discussing the elements contained in the Story Map, ask the students to complete it based on the events in **one** chapter of the literature selection. When the students are finished, divide into groups based on the chapter chosen to be mapped. Conduct a group discussion to review the information completed in the Story Map.

Invite students to complete a second story map for a different and original legend about a medieval knight. Discuss the new story maps. Exchange maps with a classmate and write a new story based on the revised map.

EVALUATION:
Can the student identify the elements of the story in order to complete a story map? Was the student able to complete a story map then use its elements to write an original story?

KNIGHTS OF THE ROUND TABLE
Story Map

Character: _____
_____

Character: _____
_____

Result: _____
_____
_____

Result: _____
_____
_____

Outcome: _____
_____

KNIGHTS OF THE ROUND TABLE

SUMMARY OF RESPONSE:
Write content-related questions to use in a mock interview with King Arthur.

OBJECTIVE:
- The student will create questions appropriate to content to ask in an interview.
- The student will answer in a manner consistent with context of story.
- The student will work cooperatively to plan and carry out a role-playing interview of King Arthur.

THINKING LEVEL:
- Comprehension
- Application
- Application

MATERIALS:
- Pencil
- Writing Paper

PREPARATION:
- Begin this lesson with a preview of what role-playing is.
- Divide students into pairs.

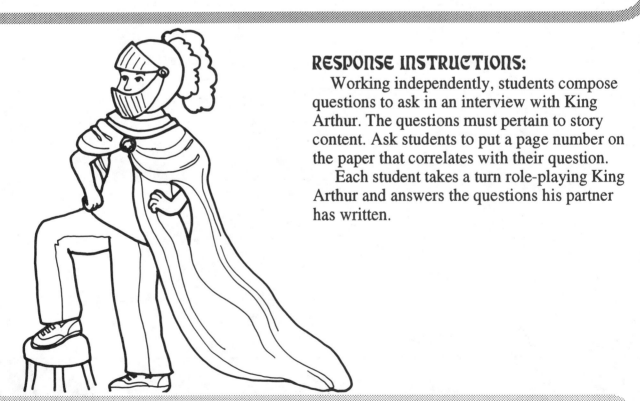

RESPONSE INSTRUCTIONS:
Working independently, students compose questions to ask in an interview with King Arthur. The questions must pertain to story content. Ask students to put a page number on the paper that correlates with their question.

Each student takes a turn role-playing King Arthur and answers the questions his partner has written.

EVALUATION:
Was the student able to formulate content-appropriate questions? Did each student plan and carry out a role-playing interview of King Arthur?

KNIGHTS OF THE ROUND TABLE

SUMMARY OF RESPONSE:
Cooperative groups propose, write and illustrate a four-sequence continuation of the story based on the book ending.

OBJECTIVE:
- The student will propose a theory about what happens to King Arthur after he sails away on the boat.
- The student will develop the theory in written form.
- The student will portray the continuation in an illustration.

THINKING LEVEL:
- Synthesis

- Synthesis
- Application

MATERIALS:
- Large sheet white construction paper
- Pencils
- Crayons

PREPARATION:
- Review the last page of the literature selection.
- Divide into cooperative groups of four.
- Distribute a sheet of construction paper to each group.

RESPONSE INSTRUCTIONS:
The end of the story leaves the reader wondering, "what if…"? Discuss King Arthur's last words and the promise they hold. Instruct the students to fold the construction paper into four equal sections. The first student writes a continuation of the story of King Arthur's life in one section. Where did he go? What has he been doing? Did he get well? Pass the paper to the next student who writes a sentence or two that continues the story based on the newly proposed story.

Continue to pass the paper until all sections are filled and each student has contributed. Decide on a title for the chapter. Illustrate each section. As a class, share different continuations.

EVALUATION:
Can the student propose a story continuation and logical plot outcomes based on the continuation? Can students compose a continuation of King Arthur's life?

Respond

KNIGHTS OF THE ROUND TABLE

SUMMARY OF RESPONSE:
Examine story content with a focus on specific information.

OBJECTIVE:
- The student will work cooperatively to discuss and come to an agreement on four questions about the text.
- The student will discuss and evaluate responses given by other cooperative groups.

THINKING LEVEL:
- Analysis
- Evaluation

MATERIALS:
- Chart paper
- Task Cards, following
- Pen or pencil

PREPARATION:
- Divide students into groups of four.
- Prepare four pieces of chart paper with one Task Card taped to the top of each.
- Distribute one prepared chart paper to each cooperative group.

RESPONSE INSTRUCTIONS:
Groups designate a recorder. Each group will get an opportunity to complete the tasks on each sheet. The students will have fifteen minutes to discuss and come to an agreement and record their response. Each response must be different from previous groups' responses.

After each group has completed all four focus tasks, place each chart paper on the chalkboard so everyone can see the responses. As a group, solicit evaluations and questions about the posted material.

EVALUATION:
Can the student work cooperatively to come to an agreement about the answer to questions regarding the text? Can the student discuss and evaluate responses given by other groups?

KNIGHTS OF THE ROUND TABLE
Task Cards

CARD NUMBER 1

Go back to the reading assignment and find two instances that a character displays emotion. What emotion is the character displaying and what is the cause? Do you think the response is appropriate?

CARD NUMBER 2

Go back to the reading assignment and find an instance in which one character treated another with fairness and justice. Describe the event briefly.

CARD NUMBER 3

Go back to the reading assignment and choose five new vocabulary words you encountered. Write each word and the page it is found on. Using your own words, create a definition for each.

CARD NUMBER 4

Go back to the reading assignment and find an example of an event or action that seems magical or unreal. Summarize the event or action in twenty words or less. Briefly explain why you don't think this part of the story could really happen.

THE DOOR IN THE WALL
by Marguerite de Angeli
Published by Dell Publishing, 1977.
Canadian distribution by Dell Publishing, Canada.

DESCRIPTION:
121 pages
Historical fiction

READING LEVEL:
Read aloud—Grades 3-4
Independent—Grades 5-7

CONTENT NOTES:

This Newbery Award Medal winner has an underlying theme of triumph of the mind over a physical handicap. Authentic historical detail is teamed with fictional text to make the pageantry and atmosphere of life in England during the Middle Ages come alive for upper grade readers. The illustrations throughout also provide readers with a glimpse of lifestyle in medieval times.

CONTENT SUMMARY:

Robin, son of the nobleman Sir John de Bureford, is expected to learn the ways of knighthood. At the age of ten, he is sent to live in the household of another knight where he will begin his training. There, Robin falls ill and loses the strength in his legs. Fearing the plague, the servants abandon him and Robin is left alone. A monk named Brother Luke rescues Robin and takes him to the hospice of St. Mark's where he is taught woodcarving. Robin becomes strong in mind and body and learns how to use crutches, for his legs continue to be useless.

Robin, Brother Luke and a Minstrel named John-go-in-the-Wynd journey to the great castle of Lindsay where, after a few days, the Welsh take over the town and the safety of the castle is in danger. But it is Robin who, unable to mount a horse and ride to battle, comes up with a plan to save the townspeople and serve his king.

THE DOOR IN THE WALL

SUMMARY OF RESPONSE:
Write a booklet that applies the theme of "doors of opportunities" to past personal experience and to predict future experience.

OBJECTIVE:
• The student will apply themes learned in literature content to past personal experience.
• The student will apply literature themes to make predictions about what future personal experience.

THINKING LEVEL:
• Application

• Synthesis

MATERIALS:
• Writing paper for students
• Chalkboard
• Chalk
• Stapler
• Half-sheet construction paper
• Crayons

PREPARATION:
• Brainstorm together and write examples of opportunities on the chalkboard: *college, summer camp, new friends, new school.*
• Fold the writing paper in half to make a mini-booklet. Cover with construction paper. Staple at the fold.

RESPONSE INSTRUCTIONS:
Several references are made in the literature selection to finding the "door". The author sends the message that everyone has doors of opportunity, but one has to search for them.

Independently, students write about one door of opportunity they have already opened and passed through. Students write how the opportunity changed their life. Students also write about a door they hope to find and open in their future. They may use the class list as a guide. They may propose what their goals are and what they want to do to encourage opportunities to come to them.

Decorate the booklet cover.

EVALUATION:
Can the student write where past and future "doors of opportunity" lead in their lives? Can students relate which opportunities would help them to reach future goals?

THE DOOR IN THE WALL

SUMMARY OF RESPONSE:
Compile a cooperative newspaper filled with articles and report on the daring rescue of Lindsay castle.

OBJECTIVE:
- The student will recall details from focused reading.
- The student will outline these details for a newspaper story.
- The student will compile details into a final written draft.

THINKING LEVEL:
- Knowledge
- Comprehension
- Synthesis

MATERIALS:
- Writing paper
- Various newspaper articles
- Reporter's Checklist, following

PREPARATION:
- Newspaper articles can be used as examples. The use of bold print and large letters in the articles can be discussed as well as the difference between fact and opinion.
- Reproduce a copy of checklist for each student.

CASTLE SAVED!

RESPONSE INSTRUCTIONS:
Students select a story angle about Robin saving Lindsay castle in order to write a newspaper article. An illustration may accompany the article.

Use the Reporter's Checklist as a first step in the writing process. Edit and proofread the article in teams. Work together to compile and publish the articles in the student newspaper. Large sheets of newsprint can serve as the "canvas" for gluing the news stories. Cooperatively determine a name for the class newspaper. Some suggestions:

Medieval Messages
Bravery Bulletin
English Tattle Tale
Days and Knights

EVALUATION:
Can the students recall details from the literature selection and write a newspaper article about the rescue of Lindsay castle? Can students cooperatively determine a newspaper name?

Respond

THE DOOR IN THE WALL
Reporter's Checklist

WHO:
Identify the important people
involved in the story.

WHAT:
Choose a specific part of
the story to retell.

WHEN:
Describe the time of this specific
event as it relates to the sequence of
the story.

WHERE:
Name the exact location where
the event you are describing
took place.

SELECT:
Select three other facts to relate.

HOW:
List the sequence or steps in the event.

THE DOOR IN THE WALL

SUMMARY OF RESPONSE:
Examine the relationship between church and state and complete a Knowlegde Web comparing the functions of medieval and present-day churches.

OBJECTIVE:
- The student will gather specific content information.
- The student will apply the gathered information to create a knowledge web.
- The student will use the web to examine the relationship between church and state.

THINKING LEVEL:
- Recall
- Application

- Evaluation

MATERIALS:
- Knowledge Web, following
- Pen or pencil
- Chalkboard
- Chalk

PREPARATION:
- Divide students into groups of four.
- Reproduce a copy of the Knowledge Web for each group.
- Discuss role churches play in modern communities.
- Reread page 25 in the literature selection.

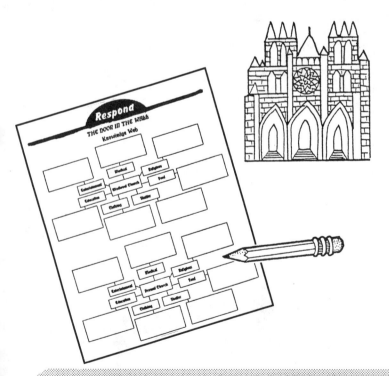

RESPONSE INSTRUCTIONS:
To spark discussion, create two separate columns on the chalkboard with the words "present church" and "medieval church" as the headings. Ask students what roles the church plays in each society. Some points to consider:

medical	religious	food
shelter	clothing	education
entertainment		

Using the information on the chalkboard, students complete each knowledge web. Group discussion should provide conclusions about the relationship between church and state during the two time periods. These can be shared with the class.

EVALUATION:
Can the student contribute to the creation of a web and examine the relationship between the church and state?

THE DOOR IN THE WALL

Knowledge Web

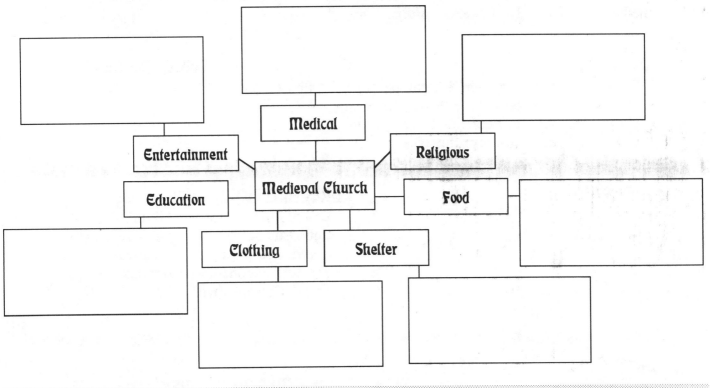

Medical

Entertainment

Religious

Education

Medieval Church

Food

Clothing

Shelter

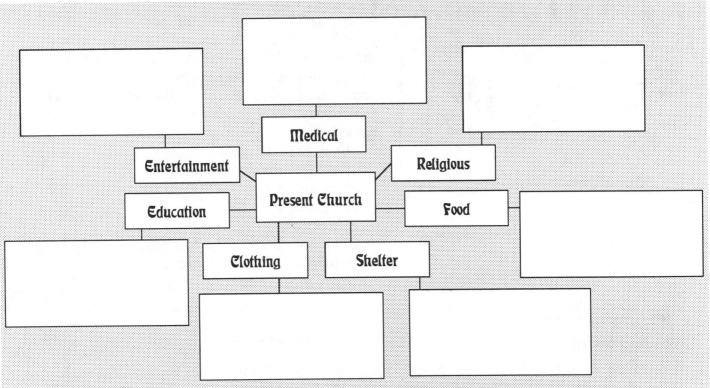

Medical

Entertainment

Religious

Education

Present Church

Food

Clothing

Shelter

THE DOOR IN THE WALL

SUMMARY OF RESPONSE:
Make a cooperative chart that compares present food safety standards to those of medieval societies. Evaluate the information.

OBJECTIVE:
- The student will contribute to a comparative chart based on story content and personal experience.
- The student will draw conclusions regarding the safety of food today and in medieval times.

THINKING LEVEL:
- Comprehension
- Evaluation

MATERIALS:
- Chart paper
- Marking pens

PREPARATION:
- Discuss the purpose and duties of the Food and Drug Administration. Why was this committee created? In what ways does it protect the consumer from unsanitary food and dangerous medicine?

RESPONSE INSTRUCTIONS:
On pages eight and nine of the literature selection, reference is made to Wat Hokester and the rotten fish he tried to sell. Create a class chart comparing food markets, stores, food preparation and where food came from in medieval times and present day. Some guidance points for students could be:

Expiration dates
Refrigeration
Wrappings
Preparation
Shipment

Guide students to come to a conclusion regarding the safety of food today and in medieval times.

EVALUATION:
Can students contribute to a class chart of food contamination safeguards for medieval times and present day? Can students come to a conclusion regarding the safety of food?

Respond

THE DOOR IN THE WALL

SUMMARY OF RESPONSE:
Use problem-solving skills to develop a plan that will save the castle that is under siege in the literature selection.

OBJECTIVE:
- The student will use problem-solving skills to develop a plan to save the castle.
- The student will present the solution orally and in a labeled diagram that reflects knowledge of story setting and characters.

THINKING LEVEL:
- Application
- Synthesis

MATERIALS:
- Student writing paper
- Pencil
- Crayons
- Large sheet construction paper

PREPARATION:
- Review the predicament facing people in the castle.
- Divide into cooperative groups. Select a group secretary.
- Give each group writing paper and construction paper.

RESPONSE INSTRUCTIONS:
Each cooperative group brainstorms plans the people may have used to save the castle. Some issues students should take into consideration are: time, unknown number of enemy, food, water, weather, weapons and outside help. Record all ideas for ten minutes. The group must select one idea that appears to be the most viable. Discuss the idea in detail.

When the solution is determined, half of the group prepares an oral description of the solution. The other half draws a diagram on construction paper that relates the sequence of the plan and labels all characters and setting details. The two presentations should be coordinated.

Present both to classmates. Follow-up with constructive evaluation of the proposed plan.

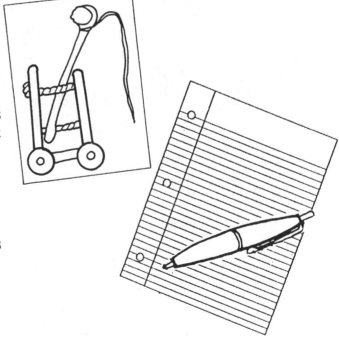

EVALUATION:
Are the students able to use problem-solving skills to develop a plan that will save the castle? Is the student able to present the plan orally to reflect knowledge of setting and characters?

THE DOOR IN THE WALL

SUMMARY OF RESPONSE:
Spend time inflicted with a handicap and assess the value of life for those who are handicapped.

OBJECTIVE:
- The student will spend time afflicted with a handicap.
- The student will use that experience to assess the value of life of handicapped and healthy people.

THINKING LEVEL:
- Application
- Evaluation

MATERIALS:
- Worksheet
- Pen or pencil
- Wheelchair, if available

PREPARATION:
- Read through page 42 in the literature selection and discuss Robin's abilities with the class. Discuss various handicaps.
- Divide into pairs.
- Reproduce and distribute worksheet to students.

Blind	Deaf
Paralyzed	Unable to talk
Lost one arm	Lost both arms
Restricted to a wheelchair	Other _____

RESPONSE INSTRUCTIONS:
After preparing students with a discussion of handicaps, assign student pairs a handicap from the box at left. Team members take turns simulating the handicap. Other team members help the afflicted person as much as possible. The simulation should last long enough for the students to experience a variety of daily tasks.

When each team has completed their turn, assign the worksheet page to be completed by each team member. Come together as a class and discuss the students' findings.

EVALUATION:
Does the student spend time afflicted with a handicap? Does the student use that experience to assess the value of life of handicapped and healthy people?

THE DOOR IN THE WALL

1. Which handicap did you have? Circle it.

   Blind   Deaf
   Paralyzed   Unable to talk
   Lost one arm   Lost right and left arm
   Restricted to a wheelchair   Other _____

2. Write a full description of your time spent afflicted with a handicap. Include how your partner helped you and some of your most frustrating experiences.

3. How would you feel if you had to depend on others in so many ways like Robin did in the story?

4. Why do you think Robin was so upset by his inability to use his legs?

5. How would having a handicap today compare with having a handicap during medieval times? What data did you use to come to this conclusion?

ADAM OF THE ROAD

by Jane Gray
Published by Scholastic, Inc., 1970.
Canadian distribution by Scholastic, Canada.

DESCRIPTION:
320 pages
Historical fiction

READING LEVEL:
Read aloud—Grade 4
Independent—Grades 5-6

CONTENT NOTES:

This Newbery Award winner gives the reader a sense of the life of a minstrel, whose home is "on the road". This tale describes many ways in which medieval childrens' lives are different from children of today, yet such common fears as being lost, losing a pet and friendship transcend time. A thorough development of the young boy, Adam, lends itself to the young reader identifying with the main character.

CONTENT SUMMARY:

Young Adam has looked forward to his dad, Roger the Minstrel, returning from France where he went to minstrel school. When Roger comes to St. Alban's to get Adam and his faithful dog, Nick, their plans for a journey begin.

Their journey with Sir Edmund and his train began well enough. Roger and Adam had Bayard, a war horse, to ride and Nick was happy to be with them. But all too soon trouble begins when Nick is stolen from Adam during the night. Roger and Adam search the town for him and during the frantic search Adam and Roger become separated!

Over miles and miles Adam travels trying to find his father. Their paths cross several times, but they just miss each other. Adam is taken in by several kind people who help him in his search. Adam shares his minstrel songs and tales with the folks he meets. This tale of loyalty and love ends with the warmth of the spring sunshine beaming down on the reunited family as they discuss traveling on the road, as minstrels should.

ADAM OF THE ROAD

SUMMARY OF RESPONSE:
Make a map of St. Alban's campus using contextual clues from the second chapter, then prioritize the importance of each building as to its function in medieval society.

OBJECTIVE:
- The student will make a map of St. Alban's campus using context clues.
- The student will classify the campus buildings in order, from least important to most important, relating to their function in society.

THINKING LEVEL:
- Comprehension
- Analysis

MATERIALS:
- Large white construction paper
- Crayons
- Pencil

PREPARATION:
- Read through chapter two of the literature selection. Focus specifically on page 21.
- Distribute a piece of large white construction paper for each student.

RESPONSE INSTRUCTIONS:
Review page 21 in which St. Alban's campus is described. List each building on the chalkboard. Ask students to make a map of the campus using the description in chapter two. Remind students to include a compass, key and scale on their map.

As a class, use the guidance questions at the right to begin a discussion about the buildings' functions on campus. These questions can be followed with individuals ordering buildings from least to most important on the back of their map. Lists can be shared with the class and reasons supporting the student's order should be discussed as well.

Guidance Questions

1. *What other buildings could be added to the campus to make a more complete "city"?*
2. *Why did St. Alban's need so many different buildings?*
3. *Are there any campuses similar to this in America today? Speculate on why or why not.*
4. *Where did St. Alban's get the funds to run such a large campus?*
5. *How important was the church and school in this society? Use evidence from the literature selection to support your answer.*

EVALUATION:
Can the student make a map of St. Alban's campus using context clues presented in chapter two? Can the student classify buildings from least important to most important?

ADAM OF THE ROAD

SUMMARY OF RESPONSE:

Participate in a class pre-reading of story elements and complete an Inference Questionnaire about author's purpose, tone and mood.

OBJECTIVE:

- The student will survey the book and infer information about the story elements.
- The student will use the table of contents, the song, the Map of the Travels of Adam and the picture on the front cover to gain insight into the author's tone, mood and purpose.

THINKING LEVEL:

- Comprehension

- Comprehension

MATERIALS:

- Inference Questionnaire, following
- Literature selection
- Pen

PREPARATION:

- Reproduce and distribute the Inference Questionnaire.
- Assign students to work in pairs.

RESPONSE INSTRUCTIONS:

Inform students about important information available without even reading the first page. In *Adam of the Road*, the front cover, table of contents, the song and Map of the Travels of Adam give many details that are helpful to know. This information is important to use while reading.

Allow student pairs to complete the Inference Questionnaire. Students can use any information gained from parts of the book before the actual text begins with chapter one. After the students complete the worksheet, discuss each question as a class. Try to come to a conclusion as to the setting, time period, author's mood, tone and purpose. Keep these conclusions in mind when reading the story. Allow time at various points in the story to review these conclusions. Do answers change as the reading is done?

EVALUATION:

Can the student survey the book and infer information about the story elements? Can the student use literature elements to complete the Inference Questionnaire?

ADAM OF THE ROAD

Inference Questionnaire

Setting:

1. Where could this story have taken place?

_____

2. From the clues given, where do you think the action took place?

_____

3. Name one place where this story could not have happened. Support your answer.

_____

Time:

1. When could this story have taken place?

_____

2. Can you guess what time of the year it is?

_____

3. How long does this story take?

_____

Author:

1. Why did the author write this story?

_____

2. What mood is the story initially presented?

_____

3. What indications does the author give about the tone of the story?

_____

Respond

ADAM OF THE ROAD

SUMMARY OF RESPONSE:
Write a conversation script between two main characters in the story. Practice and present this conversation orally.

OBJECTIVE:
- Pairs of students will assume the role of either Roger or Adam and write a conversation between them.
- The student will write a dialogue using correct punctuation.
- The student will display comprehension through oral expression.

THINKING LEVEL:
- Synthesis

- Knowledge
- Comprehension

MATERIALS:
- Conversation Script, following
- Pencil
- Tape recorder (optional)

PREPARATION:
- Divide students into cooperative pairs.
- Reproduce and distribute a copy of the conversation script to each pair of students.

RESPONSE INSTRUCTIONS:
Ask each member of the pair to choose the role of either Roger or Adam. "Adam" writes a short paragraph in the first script response space. "Roger" reads and writes a response. This continues until the conversation script is completed.

Ask students to write to each other as they think the discussion would have actually been between the two characters. Encourage them to use vocabulary and ideas in the book. They may write about observations, feelings or some other story aspect. You may request the class to write about when Adam and Roger are reunited at the end of the book.

After writing is complete, have pairs practice their dialog orally, working on expression based on the content. They may present their conversation to classmates, inviting positive feedback as to the content and expression. They may prefer to record their conversation for private listening and evaluation.

EVALUATION:
Is the student able to recreate and correctly punctuate a conversation between two characters, demonstrating content comprehension through writing and oral expression?

A Conversation script between ...

ADAM _____

_____

_____

ROGER _____

_____

_____

ADAM _____

_____

_____

ROGER _____

_____

_____

ADAM _____

_____

_____

ADAM OF THE ROAD

SUMMARY OF RESPONSE:
Use the facts presented to develop a way of communication between Adam and Roger.

OBJECTIVE:
- The student will draw conclusions from content information about the lack of efficient communication in medieval times.
- The student will use content information to develop a communication system between Roger and Adam.

THINKING LEVEL:
- Analysis

- Synthesis

MATERIALS:
- Literature selection

PREPARATION:
- Read through the literature selection.
- Divide students into triads.

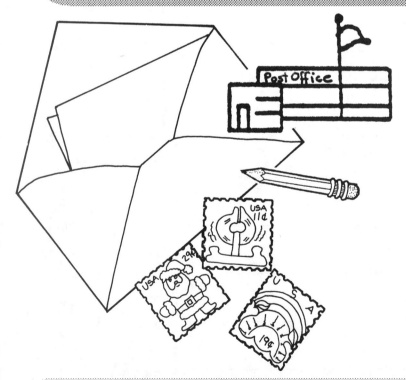

RESPONSE INSTRUCTIONS:
Begin with a whole-class activity in which details about the communication systems mentioned in the literature selection are recalled. Discuss their efficiency and encourage students to compare these to modern communication methods.

Ask each student group to use the technology available at the time and develop a way for Roger and Adam to communicate more efficiently. Each triad writes how the story might change using the newly developed system. Share these plans with the class and discuss what would result if the new communication system had been in place during medieval times.

EVALUATION:
Can the student use facts about the dilemma regarding lack of efficient communication in medieval times to develop a communication system between Roger and Adam?

ADAM OF THE ROAD

SUMMARY OF RESPONSE:
Compose a minstrel song or tale based on the audiences' interests.

OBJECTIVE:
- The student will survey the class to determine interests.
- The student will compose and present a minstrel song or tale based on this survey.

THINKING LEVEL:
- Knowledge
- Application

MATERIALS:
- Musical instruments
- Pen

PREPARATION:
- Discuss a minstrel's job. How did the minstrel decide on which songs to sing? Where did new songs come from?

RESPONSE INSTRUCTIONS:
Students create four yes or no questions regarding interests of class. Allow each student time to orally question class.

Instruct students to compose a minstrel song or tale based on the information gained through survey. The students can use the songs in the book as a guide. Have various instruments available for students to choose from. Allow each student to present the new song or tale. Ask class to give feedback as to the enjoyment level and the interest level of each minstrel song.

EVALUATION:
Does the student survey the class to determine interests? Can the student compose and present a minstrel song or tale based on this survey?

ADAM OF THE ROAD

SUMMARY OF RESPONSE:
Investigate and write a job description for medieval occupations to use in a cooperative game of charades.

OBJECTIVE:
- The student will identify medieval occupations.
- The student will describe an occupation by summarizing information.
- The student will, through dramatic play, convey the concept of an occupation.

THINKING LEVEL:
- Recall
- Comprehension
- Application

MATERIALS:
- Occupation Cards, following
- Scissors
- Pencils
- Paper bag
- Index cards
- Stapler

PREPARATION:
- Cut apart the occupation cards.
- Staple each one to an index card.
- Give an index card to each student.

RESPONSE INSTRUCTIONS:
A variety of jobs were essential in the medieval community. Many are listed on the Occupation Cards on the following page.

Each student investigates the occupation on the card they received. They write a job description for the occupation on the index card.

Place all the index cards in a paper bag. Play a game of charades. Ask a student to draw a card out of the bag and act out the occupation. No words may be used, only actions. Classmates try to guess which occupation is being portrayed.

EVALUATION:
Can the student describe an occupation by summarizing information? Does the student convey the concept of an occupation through dramatic play?

Minstrel	Priest
Monk	Porter
Abbot	Chapman
King	Miller
Plowman	Dairy Farmer
Squire	Laundry Maid
Reeve	Stable Man
Archer	Yeoman
Bailiff	Falconer
Liege	Ferryman
Knight	Carpenter

Exciting Resources TK-6 from

EDUPRESS

Learning can be fun! We guarantee it!
Join the satisfied teachers who are discovering the excitement
that our interactive, hands-on activity books and resources can
bring to your classroom—Today!

140   Classroom Kickoff $21.50
An indispensable, year-round resource
of hundreds of activities, tips & tools.

139   Super Arts & Crafts $21.50
Make art a lively, integrated experience
with over 700 imaginative projects.

134   Holiday Games $5.95
Gameboards, puzzles and easy games
to enrich & enliven holiday learning.

102   Indian Activities $4.95
Historical aids team with hands-on art
& craft projects from recyclables.

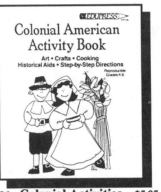

126   Colonial Activities $5.95
Experience colonial life with a lively
program of art, crafts & cooking.

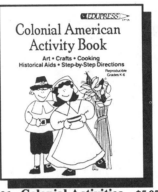

138   Frontier Activities $5.95
Art, crafts, cooking and historical aids
bring the westward movement to life.

137   Desktop Games $5.95
Skill-based individual & group games
galore for curriculum enrichment.

150 Books, Bulletin Boards $17.95
Patterns, literature links, story sparks
for student books—display tips& more!

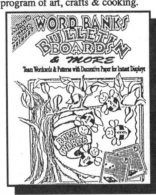

151   Word Banks & More $10.95
Ready-to-use word cards & decorative
writing paper for bulletin boards.

148 Multicurricular Starters $12.95
An idea-rich resource of over 1000
learning sparks for every subject.

130   Fall Projects $5.95
Inventive activities & themes for
September, October and November.

131   Winter Projects $5.95
Keep kids busy December, January &
February with lively themes & projects.

132   Spring Projects $5.95
Imaginative monthly theme activities
for March, April, May & June.

149   Holiday Starters $12.95
Ring in the seasons & holidays with
over 1000 learning springboards.